PRACTICAL PARENTING

PRACTICAL PARENTING

TEN BASICS THAT PRODUCE GREAT KIDS

BILL MOUNTSIER

Annotation Press (a division of WinePress Publishing, PO Box 428, Enumclaw, WA 98022) functions only as book publisher. As such, the ultimate design, content, editorial accuracy, and views expressed or implied in this work are those of the author.

ISBN 13: 978-1-59977-036-9
ISBN 10: 1-59977-036-9
Library of Congress Catalog Card Number: 2011912696

DEDICATION

This book is written in honor of my wife, Deb, and our children, Kyle and Katie. Deb is truly the leader for nearly all that is written in this book. I just organized the parenting ideas and put them into a book. She is the best parent I know and the love of my life! Kyle and Katie deserve much of the credit for the book too; if they hadn't turned out so wonderfully, I would have no right to write the book! Seriously, you have each turned out and continue to be even more than I ever could have imagined—because of our great parenting … and despite many mistakes.

CONTENTS

INTRODUCTION

PARENTING IS EVERYTHING! Well, not quite, but it's close. Think of it this way: If you could address and fix one problem in the whole world, what would it be? If you could take away all the drugs, you would still have greed, dishonesty, and hate. If you could fix education, some people would still be lazy, and others would misuse their knowledge for evil purposes. If you could tackle environmental issues, there would still be wars and crime. Even if we could rid the world of crime, people would still be rude to each other and have all kinds of relationship problems. You could make all politicians honest and willing to do the best for the people they represent ... well, maybe you can't do that.

But if parents do what is right for their children, they grow up knowing not to use drugs, appreciating education, having a good work ethic, treating others with respect, and taking care of the world in which they live. Good parenting truly can take care of many of the problems we face in our country, maybe even the world. In fact, I propose that many problems result from bad parenting. Good parenting creates good people. And good people create a good world.

And here's the best part. Good parenting is not as hard as everyone thinks. We have gotten distracted with such topics as "quality time," enrichment classes, opportunities, sports, music, a good relationship with our kids, moral issues in our communities, pros and cons of certain teachers, social adjustment, special needs ... you get the idea.

If parents would simply follow the basic directions in this book, I believe that most difficult parenting issues would fade away. By following these actions, parents will have fewer difficulties. And the difficulties that do arise will be handled more easily because the parents and the children will be working from such a strong foundation. Each chapter teaches an essential in parenting. They seem obvious. But the more I observe and talk to parents, the more I realize that many parents are not giving attention to these basics. And these basics are necessary. Each and every one of them.

Expect Consequences

If a child has no bedtime, he will lack discipline, probably won't get enough sleep (causing relationship and school problems), and will watch or participate in activities that are not age-appropriate.

If you do not play with your child, you won't have a full relationship with her, so honesty and trust will not develop—which will make the teen years exactly what everyone fears.

If the friends and activities in your child's life are not censored, your child will be learning and filling his mind with ideas and behaviors that go against what you may be trying to teach him.

The list of basics could probably be longer. But if you start with these ten, stick to them, focus, and persevere, you will have great kids—and a great relationship with your kids! And if you do these well in the early years, the later years, even the teen years, become an absolute delight!

Furthermore, these essentials are for *all* children. Whether your child is above average, below average, or just average; has special needs or is a genius; has physical limitations or is a star athlete; or is "more mature than other kids his age"; all children will benefit from parents who love them with these essentials.

Some children will be more compliant and others more difficult. Each of these basics may require some tweaking for different children, but every child can benefit from parents who use these principles.

And these essentials are for *all* parents, despite differences in economic status, education, work hours, religious background ... whatever! They also work for different families—single parents, blended families, extended families in the home ... whomever!

You, and everyone involved in your child's life, simply need to be committed to these basics and must support each other.

My wife and I both grew up in families where these principles were practiced. And we each had loving, stable families with two parents who loved us and worked hard to make sure we had the life skills to be successful. I know this is not the case for everyone reading this book. And the culture we live in today seems different than just a few short years ago when my own children were growing up.

But the essential needs of children are the same, and the people who primarily provide for those needs are still parents. No matter what your background is, how much money you have, what your education is, or how you were raised, you can be a great parent. You can break a cycle of abuse or neglect. You can learn to play with your child. You can discipline your child appropriately. *You can do it!*

Our Story

My wife and I are not anything special. We work, play, go to church, take walks, run out of money at the end of the month, get mad, try to keep up with family, have too many weeds in our yard, eat more junk food than we should … we are like many of you.

But we love our children immensely—like you—and have given great attention to each moment of their upbringing. And so we have great children!

Kyle is twenty-five, married, and lives too far away! He graduated from college, got a job, works, plays, loves, laughs, and *lives* well. Katie is twenty-two, just graduated from college, just got married, and has too many friends! She also works, plays, loves, laughs and *lives* well.

Don't get me wrong, they are not perfect, but they are wonderful! And here's the key: We *never* worried about whether they would get involved with drugs, we *never* worried about them having sex outside of marriage, let alone getting pregnant or getting someone else pregnant, we *never* worried about getting a call from the police to get our kids out of jail, and we *never* expected or got rebellion.

Oh, yeah, if you ask them, they will tell you they loved their childhood and teen years, they love our family—especially each other—and they respect us as parents, and now as friends. They even realize they are becoming much like us in their views on life, especially parenting. (They are, however, very upset that they have started using many of our lame jokes as their own.)

So after all that, maybe my wife and I *are* something special. And you can be too! Love your son, love your daughter. Keep it simple. Do the basics.

CHAPTER 1

KNOW EVERYTHING

YOUR CHILDREN SHOULD think that you can know just about everything about their lives. This is fairly easy when children are young because you should be supervising most of their lives anyway. You should be in their rooms and their toys and their bookshelves and backpacks and closets and anything else they have. This should be natural from their infancy, so it will not seem odd as they get older.

As they get older, continue this practice as much as possible—while slowly letting them have freedoms that you keep an eye on. Though you will give your children more freedom and more privacy as they get older, they should never think that their privacy is absolute.

You still have the right—and more importantly, the responsibility—to check them out when you feel something might be wrong. They should know that their room, closet, drawers, car, backpack, and clothes are theirs only as a privilege of living with you. Even if they have a job and have paid for their own clothes, or even their own car—if they live with you, you still have the responsibility to know if anything illegal, immoral, or dangerous is happening to your children or within your home or property.

I first realized the importance of this as I spoke with people about the tragedy of the Columbine shootings. In April 1999, two fourteen-year-old boys took guns to their school in Columbine, Colorado, (just outside of Denver) and shot and killed twenty of their classmates before turning the guns on themselves.

Newspeople, commentators, politicians, and entertainers all weighed in on what they thought caused this event—video games, bullies at school, the media, the goth culture, heavy metal music, Democrats, Republicans, or any number of other things. I think it was probably a combination of many factors.

What struck me most were the conversations in which people claimed there was no way the parents could have known or done anything. The parents may have been doing many things right. Teenagers can be amazingly deceptive. This is when parenting becomes intentional. We must pay attention to everything. And we must know that we have the right and the power to do something. The police found bomb-making materials in the garage; the boys had begun to wear all black all the time; their grades had steadily declined. And in the midst of this knowledge, people I spoke to said, "What were the parents supposed to do? Check out their rooms? Go through their backpacks? Ask difficult questions?" Yes! Yes! Yes!

Protect Them

When we notice something wrong with our children, we check it out. For children, even teenagers—especially teenagers—no amount of freedom and privacy is worth more than their well-being and their lives!

When children show symptoms of illness, we ask them how they feel; we check their temperature; we take them to the doctor; we feed them properly and make them drink plenty of fluids; we even keep them home from school. And we do all this even if they do not want it.

As the parents, we decide what is best for our children, particularly in extreme circumstances. This does not mean that we pick out what shirt they wear each day or whether they should play football or an instrument. But when it comes to our children's health—physical, mental, or emotional—we need to be aware and be ready to take action if we see signs of trouble. Freedom and privacy are not absolute—even for a "mature" teenager living in our home.

If my three-year-old wanders into the street and I see a car coming, I don't view this as a chance for my child to learn a lesson or for him to express his autonomy. I run to the street and get my child out of the way. I would even hand out a strong punishment in hopes that my child would not go near the street again until he learns much more about cars, bodies, and who wins. After all, that's *my* three-year-old.

Guess what? If my sixteen-year-old is in the street and is not paying attention or is mentally troubled (possibly depressed and suicidal) and I see a car coming, once again I will run into the street to save my child. I will not stand back and think:

> I've taught her all I can, and if she doesn't know better than to pay attention in the street, there is nothing more that I can do. She won't like it if I interfere with her freedom and privacy. She'll be really mad at me, and it might hurt our relationship.

How crazy is that?! I'm not going to have a relationship with her if she gets hit by the car!

So now, I see my seventeen-year-old in what looks like danger. He won't talk to me and has become secretive. He is changing the way he dresses, his mood, and his friends. He seems antisocial. His grades are down, and he doesn't care—about anything! Should I think, *He doesn't like talking to me anyway. He's probably just going through a stage. I need to respect his privacy. His room is off limits. What can I do anyway?*

No! This is my precious child. I would do anything for him. I want him to understand that life can be good—and that some choices are very bad and dangerous. I'm going to go through his stuff, talk to his teachers, and talk to his friends and his friends' parents. I'm going to do everything possible to make sure my child is not hit by this car— whether it's drugs, guns, vandalism, fights, promiscuity, or any other destructive activity. I love my child.

Because of Your Love

That is the key. This is not a parent trying to ruin a young child's or a teenager's life. This is a parent loving his or her child enough to protect that child from evil in the world or even from themselves. And that is how this needs to be communicated from a very early age. Young children will smile and even give you hugs when you explain that you love them so much, you won't let them get hurt in the street or eat something that will make them sick. And if you continue to communicate that all the way through their teen years, it will be natural for your children to appreciate you when you tell them you are always going to look out for them.

You love them so much that they will not be able to have many secrets from you. You are always allowed (not by their permission, but by your right and responsibility as the parent) to check their room, backpack, car, or anything else if you think there might be something wrong. It is your right and your loving responsibility. If done well from an early age, along with maintaining clear boundaries and loving discipline (see chapter 8), this will become an easy part of your family life—and probably not very necessary.

In our home, this has worked wonderfully well. My wife and I feel there are very few secrets that our children keep from us. You may think that we are just naïve and that our children are just like everyone else's. Certainly, we do not know everything. But trust me. Our children are not like everyone else's. They are fantastic, and they are not doing all they can to keep things from their parents. They barely mind if we have looked in their backpacks or rooms for something. And all we have looked for are permission forms or money or something else we need. (That's right, we are the ones who usually have to borrow money from our kids! Wait—it will happen to you!) We've never had to look for evidence of something bad in their lives.

The important point is that they don't mind if we look. We have no secrets, and they have no secrets. We do not use this right to look into every inch of their lives every day. We would use it only if they gave us a reason to.

This loving relationship has developed a great amount of trust, knowing that we want only the best for each other. My daughter keeps a prayer journal, and I have never read one word of it. It is hers, and I trust her because of her overall behavior. But she knows that if she starts changing her behavior drastically without a good explanation, that journal will be mine. Because, as her parents, her mother and I will *know everything* possible to keep our children safe.

Action Points

1. In natural conversation, let your child know that you love her so much that, as her parents, you are allowed and responsible to know what is going on in her life. This might include you going through her room or backpack.

2. Ask your child which friends have great parents and why. Then explain the ways you try to be a great parent.

SET A BEDTIME: THE EARLIER, THE BETTER

HAVE YOU EVER been at the store late at night—nine, ten, or even later—and seen a mom or dad carting around a young child. I see it all the time. Often, it is not a pleasant experience for anyone—the child, the parent, or those of us who have to watch. The child is crying, maybe even screaming. The parent is scolding the child for making a scene, and the child responds with more crying and screaming. The tension mounts between the two and then come the spanks, yanks on the arms, and more yelling—this time from both the parent and the child!

Yes, the parent may have had a very hard day. This may be the only time he can shop. He may be a single parent—and I marvel at what single parents are able to accomplish each day, week after week. The parent may be very tired. But this scene is not the child's fault. The child is most likely tired beyond measure. And a child is not capable of handling his emotions and body when he gets that tired. Adults—parents—are supposed to be the ones under control.

Preventive Medicine

We live in very mortal bodies. The older I get, the more I realize how trapped I am by the state of my body. I don't run, jump, play, or do just about anything like I used to (though my thumb has gotten pretty nimble on the remote).

When we watch children play, we think they have an unlimited source of energy. Some children can play for hours at a time without breathing hard or even breaking a sweat. But they can't go on forever. Eventually, they have to break down—and I mean break down. In fact, it's usually the ones who seem like they will never stop who usually lose it altogether when they get too tired. Tantrums, fits, crying, complaining, arguing, fights, and other disruptive behavior are not always just the result of hurt feelings or losing a game.

Often, they are simply the signs of a very tired child who has reached the breaking point. Most adults struggle to maintain good work (play) habits and relationships when we are tired—and we are supposed to know better and have more resources to handle these difficulties. When a child without rest reaches a point of no return, it is only natural for her to act out.

This is basically a health issue. And health affects everything we do. Our health affects our work and play, our relationships, our decision-making, our reactions, our thinking, our self-control, our psyche and spirit, our personality and disposition—really everything! And one basic need we all have is sleep. That's simply the way we are made. No one lives on one hour of sleep a night.

So make sure your children get plenty of sleep on a scheduled basis.

"A scheduled basis" means they ought to have a bedtime that is as routine as possible. Imagine if you tried to go to sleep at ten one night, eight the next night, midnight the night after that, and so on. You would not get quality sleep and would probably become cranky. To do this a couple of times might not bother you, but if you did it regularly, your health would truly suffer. For children, the problem is multiplied. A change in a child's routine of one to two hours each night can be devastating. The results are poor health, poor learning, bad behavior (which becomes a learned response in other situations as well), and poor relationships with the family and others.

Establishing a regular bedtime is especially important as children get into other regular routines, such as any kind of day care, preschool, and certainly school itself. Without proper sleep, naturally smart children will compensate in any learning activities, but they will also develop bad learning habits that will affect them later in life. And every child will experience the emotional struggles that come with being tired and needing to deal with other children and teachers. Some sleep-deprived children will develop the defense mechanisms of bullying, lying, or cheating. Others will cry, be made fun of, and sink into their own lonely world. These patterns are fallen into quickly and can follow students the rest of their lives. They can be broken, and children can be redirected into more productive lifestyles, but it is difficult.

For All Ages

The time to start with regular bedtimes is when children are very young. But don't stop there! Older children and teenagers also need a routine. Studies now show that teens need even more sleep than children. And while the sleep itself is important, so is the routine of a set bedtime. This simply provides good habits for later in life.

I understand that some situations are beyond your control. We live in a fast-growing area, so sports leagues have a hard time giving their teams court or field time. When my daughter was in the sixth grade, her basketball coach called and said their practice time was 9:00 to 10:00 P.M. on Tuesdays. At that point we considered her bedtime to be between 8:00 and 8:30. Of course we allowed her to practice with her team, but we also tried to make sure she rested that day or even took a nap. Yes, even in sixth grade she was encouraged to lie down and possibly fall asleep on those days she wouldn't get her regular sleep at night. She didn't miss out on anything, and she stayed healthy for school and for her relationships.

This is not just for young children. Proper sleep and rest become especially important for teenagers. But we all know teenagers. They want to do everything! They have sports, band, clubs, academics, jobs, and any number of other things that fill their lives. And that's without even mentioning the time they *must* spend with their friends—whether in person, on a cell phone, texting, or online! Add to the mix the need for freedom and personal responsibility and it seems like an impossible task to get a teenager to have a bedtime—let alone an early one!

This is one key area where healthy parenting at the earliest age makes parenting at a later age that much easier. We must, at an early age, build into our children's personalities, routines, and understanding the fact that proper sleep is necessary. So when they become teenagers, they accept it more easily and recognize its benefits. Just as we drill into our children that drugs are bad for them and we give them multiple reasons and state it over and over again, we must do the same with sleep habits.

SET A BEDTIME: THE EARLIER, THE BETTER

To set a proper bedtime, you need to start from the end. Consider what an appropriate bedtime will be for a senior in high school, then work backwards. Here is an example:

Junior–Senior	11:00 P.M. or 10:00 P.M.
Freshman–Sophomore	10:00 P.M. or 9:30 P.M.
7th–8th Grade	9:00 P.M.
4th–6th Grade	8:30 P.M.
1st–3rd Grade	8:00 P.M.

These are just examples (though I think they are really good ones). The important thing is to keep in mind that no child will think it is right to have his bedtime moved earlier! The most difficult age for our area is when moving from sixth grade to seventh grade, because school for seventh graders starts more than an hour earlier. This means the child is actually losing some sleep time. But there is practically no way you will convince your seventh grader that she should go to bed earlier than she did the previous year.

The point is that you should not indiscriminately start raising the bedtime year after year—or else your freshman in high school will be going to bed at midnight, and your senior at 2:00 A.M.!

Unfortunately, most children think they should be able to stay up much later—mostly because their friends stay up later. The most troubling age for this is fifth to eighth grades. These children in our culture are growing up far too quickly. They watch TV shows and movies they should not watch, and they spend more time with friends than is necessary or healthy. Primarily, this is time they should be spending with their family, especially their parents, who are still instilling values and habits to make them into the best people they can be. Their friends are not trying to do that, and they often are tearing down what you may be trying to teach your child.

So stay strong and point out the benefits of getting good sleep. As with all the disciplines in this book, state it without drama and with great love. Remember, you set a bedtime for your child because you love him, not because you are trying to ruin his life!

For weekends and non-school times, I suggest anything from a half hour to an hour later than that year's bedtime. For juniors and seniors, it might be even a little later, but there should still be a curfew and some expectation of a bedtime.

Making Adjustments

So how do we handle difficult schedules? First, recognize that the bedtime will not always work when there are practices, church or other activities, or even a parent's work schedule that demand adjustments once or twice a week. It just cannot turn into a changing time each night.

Second, make this a priority for the regular nights. Decide on a bedtime and stick with it night after night. Develop a routine and state the time and routine regularly so your child understands this is an important part of your family's life.

Finally, if your own work schedule is the problem, pay for child care for the extra half hour so you can do the shopping or whatever you need to do. This small investment will pay large dividends in the future—and even on a daily basis for your relationship with your child.

Action Points

1. Decide on appropriate bedtimes for each of your children.

2. Tell them about proper amounts of sleep and what their bedtimes will be. Even at a very young age you should talk to them, so they will be used to this and understand.

3. Talk *with* them, getting their input, about what the routine will be for the last fifteen to thirty minutes before bedtime.

4. Have an understanding about nights when bedtime will not work—practices, special outings, etc.

CHAPTER 3

FEED THEM WELL AND APPROPRIATE AMOUNTS

I LOVE SWEETS. My favorite is a Mars candy bar. For some reason, I can't seem to find those around much anymore, so I have to settle for a Snickers, or a Hershey's with almonds, or a Milky Way (especially from the freezer), or … well, you get the idea. And it doesn't have to be chocolate. I'm fine with Skittles, Starbursts, jelly beans, spice drops … and let's not forget the salty stuff like chips and nuts. I am a true junk food junky! But I don't eat this junk all the time. In fact, I rarely eat it (though not as rarely as I should). My parents taught me well; I paid attention in health class; I listen to my doctor; I can compare and contrast healthy and unhealthy people; duh!

Back to Basics

We may disagree on specific diets, but I'm fairly sure we can agree that a diet of junk food is bad for you—and that some kind of balance of grains, fruits and vegetables, dairy products, and proteins is healthier. Though there are some stories of individuals who survive on nothing but fast food, chips, and ice cream, the general population is much better off with proper amounts of "healthy" foods.

Yet it has been said that we are facing an epidemic of obesity. Far too many of us, especially our children, are unhealthy because of our lack of activity and our poor eating habits. I do not include a section in this book on appropriate amounts of play and exercise, so let me say just a word here.

Kids are supposed to play. Their bodies and their imaginations are designed to develop creative play by themselves and with friends. Though many benefits can come from good television, computers, and electronic games, those need to be secondary to a child's, or anyone's, personal creativity. I'm all for some fun and education through various media, but not much exercise happens while looking at a screen.

So get the kids out to play! For the children who still play these games, tag, capture the flag, kick the can, and hide and seek are all still favorites. And the games they make up on their own are even better. And if they can't find friends to play with, you should get out there and hide behind a tree, toss a ball, or be "It."

Now back to the food. We have become self-indulgent, and because of guilt or a lack of willpower, we indulge our children with the simple pleasures of food. It becomes the easiest way to keep them quiet, or happy, or off our nerves, or off each other's nerves, or from fighting, or complaining … you get the idea. It's a quick fix. In fact, many of us use food this way ourselves, so to be fair, we also give in to our children. That's the way our thinking goes. How can we demand good eating habits out of our children when we set a horrible example?

So first things first. If you won't do it for yourself, eat healthier for your child's sake. Think about her future as a school-age child, as a teenager, and as a young adult.

You do have the willpower to eat well and appropriate amounts. If you don't think you can, get a partner to keep you accountable, join WeightWatchers with a friend, set a short-term goal, and do something for your child's sake!

Avoid Junk

Then feed your child well and proper amounts. I won't go through all the various scenarios for each meal. Just keep it simple and to the point. Children do not need lots of sugar, so keep soft drinks to a minimum. Be radical and give them milk, fruit juice, or even water! And these high-powered drinks—Monster, Red Bull, and others—are not good for anyone, let alone children and teens.

Breakfast should be cereal, fruits, pancakes, eggs, and other similar "breakfast" foods, not Popsicles, soft drinks, and candy bars.

The traditional lunch of a sandwich or wrap, fruit or vegetables, crackers, and a small dessert is great. Snacks can be anything similar to the lunch, but make sure you don't load your children up with sweets or salty snacks like chips.

And the options for dinner are endless … as long as you include some protein and vegetables. You can read all kinds of articles, pro and con, about grains, dairy products, carbs, and every other sub-category of foods, but everyone agrees on proteins, fruits, and vegetables. So use "normal" foods and use everything in moderation.

Dinner Together

Let me also encourage you to eat these meals at home—and together as often as possible. Dinner is an especially important time to talk about the day and share life as an entire family. This gets harder as children get older with various commitments, so work hard to make it a priority whenever possible.

Even as college students, our children looked forward to Friday nights and told other friends they couldn't go out because that was the night we went out to eat as a family. Here's the kicker—we almost always went for fast food. It doesn't have to be fancy, just time together.

Variety and Limits

Try to get your child to eat as many different kinds of foods as possible. We were fortunate that our children ate just about anything, and we never experienced a picky eater. The reason for learning to eat various foods is not just a matter of health; it becomes a matter of ease in social situations. If your child eats only hot dogs and beans, it's hard to go to other people's homes for a meal. And as the child becomes a teenager, he will feel out of place in many situations with friends. So try to get them to at least try whatever is served. My wife and I have different opinions about this. We were both raised to finish everything on our plates. One of us thought this was a good practice, and the other rejected it. My wife is allowed to be wrong! No, we just continue to work it out as our children have grown to adulthood.

Finally, feed them appropriate amounts. Just because your five-year-old *can* eat a Big Mac, another hamburger, a large fries, and a large Coke, doesn't mean he should. Of course, the more he eats, the more he will be able to eat. But you can determine how much he eats from a very early age.

I know I could eat a whole bag of Oreos while watching a ball game, and my kids could too. That doesn't mean I should—or that I do. I discipline myself for my own sake—and for my kids' sake. Besides, that would get expensive.

Be careful, especially when eating out. Restaurants are notorious for serving huge portions of side items such as fries or mashed potatoes. They are relatively cheap, and it makes the customer feel like he is getting a great deal—so much food for whatever the price. Just because it is served, does not mean it needs to be eaten right then. Leave it on the plate or take it home for tomorrow's meal.

Action Points

1. Figure out how not to eat so many meals at fast food restaurants.

2. When people are at home, make eating together a priority. Don't let children eat in their rooms—and you shouldn't watch TV while others eat on their own.

CHAPTER 4

PLAY WITH THEM

CHILDREN LEARN THROUGH play. Actually, all of us learn through play—or at least participation. And we are not talking just about learning academic material; we're talking about manners, fairness, rules, sharing, and all those relationship details that make up our lives. We learn these best by doing them, and by experiencing them over and over again. Certainly talk comes into the picture at some point (see chapter 6), but it all begins with play. And we must play, or participate, with our children as much as possible, as long as possible.

Everyone jokes about sitting at a little table to have a tea party with their two- or three-year old. But this is parenting at its very best! In this scenario a child can learn about place settings (and about the order that exists in many parts of life), manners, proper English, how to serve, relational skills, balance … and best of all, trust and love for you, the parent. That's the real key. You are developing a life-long relationship based on common experiences and trust. The same thing happens when playing with trucks, playing table games, playing cops and robbers, playing cards, playing sports, playing dress-up, playing … playing … playing!

Everyone worries about what it will be like as a parent of teenagers. They expect the communication will be awful and that their teens won't trust them or talk to them about the important matters of life. But if you play with them, they will talk to you about everything. Talking, communication, and trust all begin with playing—entering into their world. And for a child, playing *is* their world. If you are willing to do that, they will talk to you about everything, because you have gained their trust in their world.

Values

Play is an excellent time for teaching also. Certainly, if you are playing a game, whether it is a board game with older children or tag with younger children, rules and fairness are important. These are easily transferred to other parts of life. Schools, business, government, and relationships all have rules – written and unwritten. Even when we don't understand why, there are usually good reasons for the rules. Cheating hurts someone, and eventually that someone is the one who cheats.

Safety for each person is significant. That's why there are boundaries like not going into the street or over the hillside. These rules are similar to "rules" in life that are there for our own protection as well as for the safety of everyone else.

Ownership and sharing are significant in life and we begin to learn these in play. *Sharing* is a key word for preschoolers. But they should also be learning the value of owning things for themselves and for others. As much as we talk about sharing with young children, in real adult life, there is much more concern for ownership and proper sharing. As children get older, this needs to be more a part of the conversations we have with them.

With ownership, even of a toy, comes responsibility. When we use our own toys and equipment, and those that belong to others, children need to be taught how to take care of these things. That means playing properly with them, putting them away, and knowing what to do when they break or are lost.

So many values can be taught and passed on through play. Think of the teaching points about fairness, teamwork, hard work, practice, bullying, winning and losing attitudes, encouragement, failure and trying again, leadership, communication, goals, respect ... all of these values and more are learned while playing. Many times they are learned through talking after the playing, but mostly they are "caught" while children play. Video games and television don't even come close to the value of play with others.

Enter Their World

Begin the habit of playing as early as possible and continue to play with them at each age level. So you crawl with your baby and do lots of face to face sounds and silliness with your infant. You do dolls, toys, trucks, dirt, and dress-up with your preschooler. You play school, real games, sports, music, bikes, tag, Brownies, Cub Scouts, cooking, and so much more with school-age kids.

My wife and I took our dog for a walk the other day and saw a young family we dearly love. The dad was playing tag in the backyard with their seven-year-old son and their four-year-old daughter. (Mom was taking care of the baby!) When we yelled to them, they stopped and each said, "Not It!" So I was It for about one minute until I ran out of breath. As we talked for a short time with the parents and the children, the daughter begged her dad to go practice their dance. With no embarrassment, the dad was ready and willing—and even did a little of the dance for us right there. Way to go, dad!

There is a public service announcement on television right now that shows an overweight, balding guy doing cheerleading moves to some music. He looks pretty ridiculous until the camera pans away and shows his nine- or ten-year-old daughter next to him doing the same routine. She stops the music, starts it again, and says, "Dad, let's do it again!" With no hesitation, they start up again, and there is no doubt that the dad's heart is fully into that routine—because his heart is fully into his daughter!

Then, as your children are in fifth through eighth grades, you still play with them all you can. But if they have their own things—dance, tumbling, science projects, soccer, or anything else with which you feel totally inept—you still stay as close as possible. Try to participate with them. But if you can't, go to the practice and watch (just don't do work while you are there), then ask all kinds of questions. Be as excited as they are about whatever they are into.

Ways to Connect

It gets even tougher when they enter high school and their interests may be totally different from yours. They will know that. But if you connect in any way possible, they won't care. Your love will shine through your presence and your interest in their lives. And that is what teens so desperately want and need—to know they are loved, no matter what their interests.

I still call this playing, because you are entering into your child's life, his or her world. It is critical at each stage of a child's life because it builds trust that leads to talking—communication. You've probably heard that communication is important in any relationship.

And playing should begin from day one—as soon as you possibly can! Don't wait until they are teenagers, and then try to enter their lives just because you think that age is more important. By then, they have figured out whether you are truly interested in them. The trust that playing creates is built over time.

Many parents fear, even while their child is young, that when he becomes a teenager, he won't communicate with them and trust them, and will eventually rebel. The parents give them all kinds of material things, but never give themselves to their child through play and participation with him. So when he becomes a teenager, the parents' fears are realized because the teenager has figured out there is no real relationship. You must enter your child's life—over and over again, day after day.

Even if you are the type of person who relates better to middle-school children or teenagers, you cannot wait until then to start relating to your children. You have to break out of your personality, get down on the floor, and play trucks … *vrrrmmm, vrrrmmm*. And then you have to go to the tea party and enjoy some apple juice … made especially for you!

If you are reading this and your children are already at an age where they are noticing that something is wrong and that you need to change things, read the appendix in the back of the book! You can start now. It will just take a little more work.

Action Points

1. For younger children, each parent needs to spend at least thirty minutes each day you are with your child doing what your child enjoys.

2. For older children, plan to do at least one special activity with each child this week. You do not have to tell your child about "your plan." Just do it!

CHAPTER 5

READ WITH THEM

I DON'T LIKE to read. I never have, and I don't think I ever will. I have to force myself to read most things—even for my work, and even for things I am really interested in. (I realize I am asking you to read this. Believe me, I'd rather be doing this by a live presentation—it's a lot more fun for me … and probably for you, too!) But because I love my children, I have always read with them.

The benefits of reading together are tremendous. First, reading together provides great intimacy. As your children sit in your lap or close to you, trust and love grow in a way that only gentle physical touch can provide. I'm guessing (hoping) your fourteen-year-old won't be sitting on your lap. But the closeness you develop in their young years will carry through in significant ways.

Second, reading as a regular, daily activity helps your child learn. Whether the reading is fantasy, animal life, about families, or anything, your child will learn vocabulary, speech, sentences, and facts about whatever you are reading. Young children—as well as older children and pre-teens—have a tremendous capacity for learning and memory. They pick up things that adults miss all the time.

Third, even more important than the facts they may learn, they will develop a habit of reading—and, hopefully, a love for reading that will help them not only throughout their education, but also for their whole lives. The overwhelming evidence shows that readers are better learners and enjoy more productive lives. This is simple academics. Yes, I could add music, art, numbers, and all kinds of other academic ideals. But the one you cannot do without is reading.

Fourth, reading will develop your child's imagination and thinking. As stories unfold, your child's mind will be filled with ideas, possibilities, problem-solving, and questions. This will certainly happen during the reading, but those abilities will also be developed for other times, such as interacting with family or friends, playing with toys, doing chores, or even for those *very short times* when your child is allowed to watch age-appropriate television or videos. Reading makes all other activities easier and more enjoyable.

Read, then Discuss

And finally, when their minds are stimulated so wonderfully, they will want to ask questions and talk with you about what they are reading—or wherever their minds take them. Again, this is critical for your ongoing parent-child relationship of love and trust. And if this starts from the very beginning of their lives, they will continue to talk to you about everything right through their teen years and even as they become adults.

So read with them about everything—science, cultures, fantasy, people, families, where babies come from, God, how things are made, history—everything!

And keep reading with them. When they are old enough to read on their own, sit right with them as they read to you. Enter into the fantasies and stories with oohs and aahs and animal sounds. Ask questions about what they read so you can engage them in conversation and thought. Even after they learn how to read, make sure you still read to them sometimes. This will allow them to enjoy the stories and let their minds work without having to labor on the process of reading.

And as they get even older, still read some things together. If they have a book assigned in fifth grade (or tenth grade!) you can read the book also, then have a good dialogue about it. Don't get too deep; they will think they are in school with you also! But just a few remarks back and forth will give you a common experience and show your children your interest in all they do—that's your love for them.

Do not put your emphasis on how well they do on the paper or the test (though you need to do some of that). Instead, concentrate on simply showing your interest in their life.

Action Points

1. Read the newspaper comics with your children— even if they are too young to understand them.

2. Read a chapter of a fictional story each night to your younger children just before bedtime.

3. Ask your teenager what book he has to read for English, what the book is about, and whether or not he likes it.

TALK WITH THEM

THIS IS THE activity where so much happens. Yes, playing with your children and reading with them are important in themselves, but one of the great results is that these activities lead to talking with them. The older they get, the harder it is to play and read with them, so your communication becomes paramount. This is evident in the statements you often hear such as, "My parents don't understand me," "My teen never talks to me," and "I don't know what to do."

So how and when do we talk to our children? Start now! The younger, the better. But even if you have a teenager, start right now. The more you get her used to talking to you, the more she will accept that talking to you is normal.

If your young children learn to tell you everything about their day at school, about friends, about feelings, about teachers, and about what they like and don't like, they will continue to tell you as they get older—even in their teen years.

This is critical. They should be talking with you about all the important things in their lives, and especially as they go through the most difficult times. Often these happen in the teen years. But children can also experience some very difficult times in younger years, so communication is important at every age. Plus, if you don't talk to them about everything when they are young, they won't know how to talk to you in their teen years. You will not have built up trust and communication skills for your unique relationship with your child. So get started—and continue at every age.

Digging In

This may take some work. First, you need to help your children talk to you. Ask lots of questions.

Except that our son loved everything, he was typical of many boys as he grew up. We would have to help him talk about it.

When he said school was great, we would have to ask him what was so great.

He would usually just say, "Everything!"

So then the work started. "What did you do in math? Whom did you play with at recess? Did you do an experiment in science? How was the spelling test? Did you get the part in the play? How do you feel about that? Do you talk to Jason anymore? Why isn't he your friend now?" And more and more questions.

The more you do this, the more they will learn to talk about everything that is going on in their lives and will trust you with this information (more on this later).

Second, you have to be willing and actually be interested to hear about how they put the glue on the paper, and then the glitter, and act like it is the most wonderful event in their lives—because for them it is! You have to listen and care about your child not getting to sit next to his friend for ten minutes during reading time. You have to listen to how to play a game she made up that makes no sense at all. You have to listen to your son explain who makes the best fart sounds with his armpits (and then explain that is appropriate only at certain times and in certain places). You have to listen to your daughter explain how her friend made a face at her and that they will never talk again.

And through all this, you need to be truly interested.

Sometimes, that means sitting and looking them in the eye and asking follow-up questions. Especially when they are excited about something, they want you to be just as excited and fully engaged.

Earning the Privilege

Other times, the important talk happens as you are getting their snack ready, doing the dishes, driving somewhere, or playing together. Sometimes the most intense conversations will take place not while you are eye to eye, but in a more relaxed atmosphere. For younger children especially, they don't need to feel like any trauma or difficult situation is going to scar them forever. So you need to take it seriously, but not act as though it is the first time it has happened in the history of the world.

Then you have earned the privilege of hearing about school issues, boyfriends and girlfriends, bullying, making or not making the team, or about play, self-image, friendships, teachers, the dance, peer pressure, hopes and dreams, anger, sadness, joy … everything!

This should be every parent's goal. Because if your children are sharing all this with you, it means that they trust you and value your interest in their lives. And that means they will also value your opinion!

Then you get to direct, advise, and love them through both the great times and the difficult times. This is the right, the responsibility, the privilege, and the joy of parenting. Do you want them to get this advice from peers, from other adults you may not know, or worse, from TV, movies, and Hollywood stars whose lives are often a mess? No! This is your child, and so it is your job and your joy.

Notice that you are supposed to talk *with* them—and not *to* or *at* them. In fact, you may have noticed that most of your job is getting them to talk to you. Your primary role is to listen. A famous quote says we were given two ears and only one mouth for a reason.

Through much listening you will earn the right to talk . . . and be listened to. Many parents talk a lot, forcing their children to hear, but their children are not listening in a way that matters. So make sure the talking begins with them. What they say will often be much more important than what we say (as wise as we are), because it is that direction of talking that builds the trust.

Appropriate Answers

What should we talk with our children about? Everything! You should talk about everything they want to talk about, with attention to their age and what is appropriate then. But if they bring it up, you better be willing to talk about it to a certain extent. That can entail: dirt, bugs, toys, where babies come from, body parts, bodily functions, food, animals, scary things, boogers, shaving, sex, sports, weather, politics, work, school, music, TV, kissing, cuss words, feelings, friends, money, family ... you get the idea.

Be sure not to share more information than they need or can handle. Your six-year-old doesn't need to know how much money you lost when the stock market crashed, how cows are slaughtered to make her Happy Meal, or all the details of making love. Still, you should be as honest as possible. Most children can handle difficulties as long as they see how well you are coping with them. You can tell them that someone has died. It is sad and we don't think we will die soon, but it is OK. This is a good reason to live well every day! "The hurricane was terrible and Uncle Joe and Aunt Betty's house was hit hard, but they have dealt with other problems and they will make it through this also."

"The Talk"

When my son was about seven, we had a most wonderful short conversation. I can still picture driving with him next to me in the front seat. We had talked about babies growing in mommies' tummies before and the miracle of how God puts that baby there when a husband and a wife love each other. (Later talks would deal, age appropriately, with the process of pregnancy.)

So Kyle says, "The baby starts off real small and grows bigger in Mommy's tummy, right?"

"That's right, Kyle," I said.

Then the question came: "Is it kind of like an egg?"

Now that's a question I can handle. "Well, Kyle. In fact that's exactly what we call it at first. It's an egg." Then I sat anxiously, waiting for the next question as Kyle stared out the window. Finally he said, "There's just so much for a kid to wonder about!"

"Yes, there is, Kyle." *Whew!* Breathe. Breathe. Breathe. That was it! That's all he needed to know, and he didn't even know what to ask next—so I didn't need to jump the gun and explain it all.

Unfortunately, our real discussion about sex came in fourth grade. We explained it all using the proper language, in a matter-of-fact way, but also explaining why it is important that only married people do this. I say "unfortunately" because I don't think that fourth-graders need to be concerned about this. But three issues forced the conversation.

First, the "F" word is now used by so many people, including fourth-graders. I want my children to learn from me what difficult words mean and why they are inappropriate—not from another fourth-grader who obviously hasn't been taught. Second, so many children are not being monitored and they are free to watch R-rated movies. Again, I don't want my children learning from other children who are not being raised well. And finally, sex has come to the elementary school. Yes, sixth-grade girls are approached by "cool" eighth- and ninth-graders to be girlfriends, and then are led into sexual activity.

So start young and make it as natural as possible. Then, when the more difficult parts of the discussion come up, your child will already have a foundation of talking with you and will naturally talk about this also. Concerning this subject, there are also many good books for various age levels that can help you start the conversation.

Listen more than talk. Listen with great interest. Talk about everything. And always remain calm. Nothing should be such a surprise that you react in a way that overwhelms your child.

Reacting Reasonably

Take the lead in showing your child how to respond to various aspects of life. If your child brings up a subject you don't feel comfortable talking about or think he shouldn't be asking about—and you respond that way—he will most likely never approach you about that subject again.

If your only response is, "Don't you ever say that word again!" your child will either learn that you are naïve and don't understand the world or he will learn how to push your buttons. If you yell and scream, your child will yell and scream. If you react with compassion, concern, righteous indignation, laughter, reason—whatever is appropriate—he will learn to react in the same way.

And here is the beauty of talking together: If you have gained your children's trust, through listening, caring, interest, and love, then you will get to influence them concerning the big issues of morals and values. Through your example (see chapter 10) and through talking, children take on your values. But it needs to be done in a respectful and loving manner. Talking life out—in the midst of play, reading, and all of life's experiences—is how we internalize the values we develop. So become involved with your child's life, at every age, and learn to talk about all of it.

Action Points

1. Ask your children: If money were not a concern, what would be the best one-month vacation they could imagine?

2. Have your young children draw a picture and then tell you a story that involves that picture. Ask lots of questions—and listen.

3. Have a contest with your teenager to see who can tell the most things about yourselves in just two minutes. Afterward, ask questions about what you heard.

CHAPTER 7

SHOW YOUR LOVE TO THEM
(This chapter should be read in balance with the next chapter!)

I AM ASSUMING that you love your children. Without this love—unconditional and sacrificial—this is all a waste of time. If you do not love them, you will succumb to selfishness and take the easy way out of any difficult circumstances. This is not to say there are not times when your children frustrate you, when you can't figure out what to do, when you want to yell at them, or when you can't imagine that they are really your children. All of us run into those times. But it's important to remind ourselves in the toughest of times that we love them, so we can do the right thing for their overall well-being, and so they can become the people we want them to be.

So we all love our children. But it really is not enough just to love them—we must *show them* we love them. How else will they know? Because we all have different personalities and were raised in different ways, we don't all express that love in the same way, with the same enthusiasm—or, sadly, at all.

In today's world, it is critically important that we express our love for our children—over and over again. Children are getting messages from everywhere—music, media, friends—that say they are not worthy of love unless they dress, act, smell, and look a certain way. The knowledge that so many of their friends have divorced parents is reason enough for some children to think that maybe some day their parents will leave them. So if you are already divorced, it is essential that you reinforce your love for your children. The world can be very cruel; children (and adults!) need to have someone they can always depend on—and that comes from knowing they are loved. And to know this love, it must be expressed to them.

I watched a Little League World Series game just last night. A young boy hit a home run to put his team ahead, and the TV cameras zoomed in on his face while he rounded the bases. He had that look of a major leaguer that says, "I'm just doing my job. There's still more game to play. This is serious." No smile, no elation. Even when he hit home plate with his teammates jumping, hitting him on the head, and cheering like crazy, he was all business. Then the camera followed him back to the dugout. It was then that he looked into the stands to find his parents. When he saw them cheering and jumping, he broke into a huge smile, jumped up and down, and pumped his fists in the air. Children can have lots of friends, even friends who love them. But it is the approval and love of their parents that can make or break them.

Time Together

So *how* do we express this love? Four ways. First, you have to be with them. The catch-phrase for my generation has been "quality time." I believe that "quality" is great—talking about important issues, making memories through vacations or special outings, family nights, or date night with your kids. But the best "quality" time is "quantity" time. Watching TV together counts; reading in the same room counts; taking a walk together counts; eating a meal together counts; watching their performance at school counts; attending their ballgame counts; being home when they go to bed counts; calling them on the phone just to say, "Hi" counts a lot. Any time you can spend with them is great—and far better than one little "special" time during the week.

Someone explained it to me this way. As a guy, which would I want: one bite of the best prime rib ever or three hamburgers? It's a no-brainer—three hamburgers. I would even take just one, especially if I was hungry. So if I am hungry for love, I want a good dose of normal love, not just a little special love. And then if I am getting the regular love (the hamburgers) and you throw in a steak (special love) once a week, I am really blessed!

Here's the beauty of giving quantity love by being there: it doesn't cost anything. I am not talking about giving flowers or presents or taking them to the amusement park. Those are the special extras. What children desperately need doesn't cost anything—it's *you*!

Verbal Expressions

Second, you need to verbalize your love for them. A generation ago, this was not needed as much. While the culture was a little less verbal about affection, it was also more stable. Divorce was less prevalent, and the media did not question parents' love for their children over and over again. But children today are faced with friends who think it is perfectly normal for their parents to be divorced and for them not to have much of a relationship with their parents. The news, as well as television and movies, seems to question family relationships all the time. So children today, more than ever, need to be assured of their parents' love for them.

This means more than just saying, "I love you," though those words are most important. Affirm your children in many areas. Affirm them when they show kindness, when they get good grades, when their hair looks nice, when they clean their room or help with home chores, when they play a good game or just have a good practice, when they try their best, when they do something they didn't want to do just because they should, when they share their toys, when they obey you, when they do what they should even without your telling them, when they are polite—affirm them every day.

Tell them you appreciate what they have done *and* that you love who they are. And possibly more important, tell them of your love for them when they do something wrong. In the next chapter, we will talk about discipline, which is also a part of your love for them. It's especially important that they understand how much you love them, even when they are being disciplined. So, over and over, you need to verbalize your love for your children.

Telling Others

Third, verbalize your love for your children … to other people! Talk about how great your kids are to your friends, co-workers, neighbors, your children's friends … anyone you can make listen! This will accomplish two things. First, it will inevitably get back to your children. Other adults and children will tell your children how you brag about them.

It's one thing to hear your parents tell you how much you love them. They might expect that. But it's a big deal to hear another person tell you how your parents have been bragging about you or how much they love you. That's when you really know it's real.

Second, it will reinforce in your own mind how much you love your children. All of us get frustrated with our children at various times. This is natural and necessary. When they are not who they should be, we should be upset and even take corrective action (see the next chapter). We tend to believe what we say and think about repeatedly. If we are always talking negatively about our children, we will convince ourselves that we don't love them as much as we want to. And that will certainly show in how we act and react with them. But if we speak well of them often, we will remind ourselves how great our kids are and how much we do love them. And that will be evident in our relationships with them.

Affirming Touch

And finally, be physical with them. Shake his hand; give her a hug; kiss him on top of his forehead; push each other around; wrestle with each other; hold hands when they are young—and in our culture, even moms with sons and dads with daughters when they are older (if they're comfortable with it); have him sit on your lap; let her rest on you while watching TV together; tickle him; brush her hair … do whatever you can to have appropriate physical contact with your child. Of course, you must always be appropriate—nothing even remotely associated with physical or sexual abuse. Make sure your child feels completely comfortable with this attention. All children are not alike, and there are certainly many who will not crave or appreciate this form of love.

But when something really bad happens, almost everyone needs a hug, a touch, or simply to be held. And the best place to get that is from one's parents. Here's why: Some people in your children's lives will use that hug to get something else—information, trust, power, and even sex. I even believe many "supportive" friends of teenagers mean well when they first give a physical touch to comfort their friend. But the false trust that is built into that moment can be used by our innate selfishness to do harm later.

In this context, we are talking about loving our children as we still have influence over them because of their age. Our culture is full of young girls (getting younger every generation) who find the touch of a young man so comforting because they do not get appropriate touch from their fathers. Unfortunately, that touch from peers and older teens turns into sex so quickly, and our daughters lose their identities.

So make sure your children find their comfort, strength, security, encouragement, safety, and love primarily in your arms and from simple touches.

Tangible Rewards

I must say a quick word about gifts—money and otherwise. There is much debate about giving rewards for good behavior, achievements, good grades, etc. I believe that physical rewards ought to be given to very young children because that is the way they best understand that they have done something right. But you ought to wean your children from the need of those rewards. As they get older your words should become all the approval they need. If this is done well from an early age, children will not depend on the physical rewards as they get older. Still, children can be very different, and my wife and I may have gotten lucky with ours. Yet if your teens are still performing in school only if you've promised five, ten, or fifty dollars, something is wrong.

The other problem with gifts goes back to one of this book's premises—that all these parenting essentials can be done with little or no expense. Many parenting gurus suggest special moments like a pony ride, dinner at the child's favorite restaurant, some special gift, and so on. These are great ... for upper middle-class families who can afford it. Most people cannot afford these special treats ... *and don't need to!* Also, for wealthy parents, I have often seen this become the only form of love they have time or energy to give—and worse, the only kind the child wants to receive. This is a dangerous practice. Should you give your children gifts? Yes! Just don't let them become your primary love language to your child. I recommend time, words, and touch.

Action Points

1. Write down one thing each day that you like about your child. After a week, give the list to your child as you tell her about each item.

2. Call or text your child just to say, "Hi," and ask how his day is going.

DISCIPLINE THEM
(This chapter should be read in balance with the previous chapter!)

ET'S BE VERY clear: *Discipline is a significant part of loving your child!* Its goal is not punishment; it is about helping your child grow into the person he should be. If we think of discipline as a form of love, we'll find it easier to follow through with discipline and easier to control it so we do not react in anger.

Discipline should never be given out of anger. That emotion can get any of us. My children were mostly very good. And I think of myself as a fairly self-controlled adult. Yet I experienced a few times with my children when I could feel my anger welling up to the point that I wanted to act out—on them!

I mostly remember this happening when they were very young. It was not bad behavior that made me so mad; it was their crying. And Deb and I could not figure out the reason. Which, of course, meant more annoying crying. I remember holding my children and wanting to throw them against the wall because I could not calm them. Fortunately, I never did. And fortunately, their behavior was never so bad that it drove me to want to hit them, slap them, or abuse them in any way. We all face these moments. Please develop your self-control and see your discipline as correction, not punishment. I hope the ideas that follow will help.

Explain Why

First, always explain why you are disciplining them. Your child needs to know exactly what he has done wrong. And if you can't explain it, then maybe you are just frustrated and taking it out on him.

You may be trying to do some work, and your child is watching television in the same room. You may get frustrated and tell your child to go to his room. When he asks why, you just say, "Because I said so. Stop arguing with me!" If your TV room is the only one where you can work, you may want to talk to your child more calmly and explain the situation. If he argues, then it is fine to answer, in a calm voice, "I'm sorry, son. I know you like to watch this show, but I really have to get this work done. So I have to insist that you turn off the television now. I'll remember this and try to make it up to you another time." And then you better make it up to him.

Always explain to your children the reason for their discipline. This will help them clearly understand the rules and expectations. And more importantly, the discipline means you are serious about those rules and expectations.

Explanation combined with discipline creates learning and a much better chance for appropriate behavior. Without explanation, you can get a confused and frustrated child. Without the discipline, you will have chaos. Can you imagine a foul called in a sporting event without any consequences—without discipline? "Sir, you are not allowed to hit the guy when he is shooting. Don't do that next time. But since you got the ball, just go ahead and keep playing." That would turn out to be some game! Or think about a thief being caught. "Sir, you are not allowed to rob banks. Now give the money back and then you can go on your way. Hey, didn't I stop you just yesterday for the same thing?!" Or how about a worker? "Hey, Joe, did you get that job done that I asked you about last week? No? You've been on Facebook most of the week? OK. Just let me know when it's ready. And are you still skipping work tomorrow to go see that movie premiere?"

Our nature is to get away with whatever we can get away with. But with good direction and discipline, we can re-train our nature, then understand and internalize the attitudes and behaviors that lead to productive, contented lives.

Explain What

Second, explain what the discipline will be. Your child deserves to know. He will most likely do better with the discipline by knowing what it is than being left in a state of wonder. How long will the toy be taken away? How long will he stay in time out? It will be just one spank. What is he grounded from—and for how long? Later in this chapter you'll find suggestions on what you should use as discipline.

Explaining *why* and *what* also serves another important purpose. It gives you time to settle down, control yourself, and think through appropriate discipline and the best way to talk through it. Remember, discipline is a key teaching time and a great time to show your love to your child.

"Caleb, I just saw you take that toy from your sister. I know you think she had it for a long time, but you didn't even ask her for it. And we do not just grab things from other people. If you do this as you get older, you won't have any friends. And friends are good! So I need to put you in time out for four minutes. Go sit in the chair in the corner until I call you. Then maybe we can figure out a good way to share toys with your sister and other friends."

Discipline is teaching and loving. Don't forget it!

Key Exceptions

There are a couple of exceptions to what I just said. First, when a child, especially a young child, is about to do something truly dangerous, then a quick grab, a slap on the hand, a sharp raised voice, whatever … is needed to keep her from danger. This is for when a child is about to touch a hot burner, run into the street, jump from a dangerous height, or hit someone. Discipline quickly to save her, or her friend, then explain with possible further discipline.

Second, for older children and teens who do something extremely bad that they know is wrong, then the discipline can be indefinite. You can decide when they have "paid the price" and hopefully "learned their lesson." If you set a time limit, they may start to think that some of their bad behavior is worth the consequences. If they have been grounded for a week for missing a curfew, they may think on any given Friday night that the party is just too good to leave and that it is worth staying an extra hour. At that point, two weeks of grounding, or maybe three or four, will be needed. Only you can tell when that time is adequate.

As children enter the teen years (and even ages eleven or twelve), consequences need to be more creative and changing so the child will not want to know what you might choose next. Once, one of my children (remember, our children were really quite good) asked what would happen if they broke a certain rule. I can't remember what it was, but it was not a significant "crime." But just the fact that they were trying to figure out whether it was "worth it" brought this response: "No TV for a year!" Normally that would be too severe a discipline for a small matter. But I never wanted my children to think that bad behavior would be a viable option depending on the consequences. If they are even considering it, maybe the discipline has not been making its point.

Appropriate Timing

Third, the younger the child, the more immediate the discipline should be. You can explain all you want, but a three-year-old will not understand the connection between throwing a tantrum at ten in the morning and no ice cream after dinner. But a teen who has to miss the party this weekend or the concert in two weeks because of disrespectful behavior will get the message clearly.

Heart and Spirit

Now, how to discipline. There is one overriding principle: *The discipline must reach their heart, but not damage their spirit.* Here is what I mean. The discipline must be something that "hurts" their heart—it has to affect them at the emotional level. It needs to make them mad or sad enough that they think about their own behavior the next time an opportunity comes up to do the wrong thing. Most importantly, the discipline needs to come from the person who loves them the most—*you!* We hear stories of children who got in trouble in school, then got in even more trouble when they got home for whatever the problem was at school. This is not just about a consequence for the wrong behavior; it is about *you* training them to be the people they should be.

But the discipline should never damage their spirit. If the discipline becomes too harsh, the child will resent you.

If that happens, they are not learning anything and they lose total respect for you, destroying your relationship with them. This is a terrible situation and can produce the most rebellious of children.

Yet as bad as this can be, this is not the problem we tend to have in our society. Many parents are so afraid of damaging their relationship that they avoid any significant disciplining at all. We do not have nearly as many rebellious people as we have coddled, disrespectful "babies" who have never received the slightest reprimand. So when something does not go their way, these people blame others, quit, or cheat or try to hurt others.

So certainly do not be too harsh and damage a child's spirit. But the greater warning is to be sure your discipline is enough to reach your child's heart.

Adjusting by Age

So what "hurts" their heart? For young children, eighteen months to six to eight years old, a spank is very effective. I said "a" spank. That means *one*! Most children this age respond quickly to physical pleasure or pain. This is especially true if there is a good amount of anticipation involved—from the explanation. If you tell a child you have to spank him, then go on to explain why and how you hate to do it—and how awful it is that he has to be spanked—often the child will be nearly in tears before you even spank him, and a light touch to the bottom just puts him over the edge.

But many of you oppose spanking. So for young children, "time out" is a great way to get their attention. Simply taking away one toy allows them to move on to something else. But a "time out"—in the corner, on the step, in their room—takes them away from everything. And make sure they stay. (I recommend the show *SuperNanny* for various specifics and to show the perseverance you will need.)

You may even have to stay with your child in time out! Our daughter was a feisty child. She did not respond to spanks, she would enjoy playing in her room, and she even loved looking around while just sitting in a "time out" chair.

Finally, we placed a wooden chair facing the corner, and we would put her in the chair and tell her to face the corner. She inevitably would look around, so I would then go over, stand behind her, and hold her head facing the corner. You would have thought I was beating her! Time outs did not have to last very long—and her behavior improved dramatically and quickly. Creativity! We finally found what reached her heart!

For middle children, six- to eleven-year-olds, spanking should not be used. It becomes demeaning and demoralizing for this age child. And it obviously has not worked. At this age, time outs may still work. But most children at this age can find things to think about through even a long time out.

So that is the time to start withholding favorite items or activities. Think of all the possibilities: a favorite toy; all toys; television time; computer time; Playstation, Wii, or other gaming devices; outdoor play; friend time; going to the pool, waterpark, or amusement park; dessert; snacks; arts and crafts; cell phones (though I truly don't think children this age should have a cell phone); sitting out a game of soccer or baseball in which they are supposed to play (but make them go to the game and cheer on their team); earlier bedtime for one or multiple nights … the list is endless.

But remember, it must be something that will reach his heart, and it must be done in such a way that it makes an impact. If you take away television for the night but he is just as happy playing on the computer, the discipline has no effect. So these disciplines are usually longer and may involve multiple items. The goal is to make your child not want to do the behavior that led to the discipline in the first place. And the discipline must reach his heart so the next time the opportunity comes up, he will remember and choose wisely.

For twelve-year-olds and teenagers, the same principle applies as for older children. Only now, you may need to be even more creative and use even longer periods of time. For most young people, media and friends are the keys to their hearts—cell phones, computers (especially Facebook and other social media networks), music, movies, television, and time with friends. A few introverts will still need to be affected by other means, but most will have a near-death experience if you take away these pop culture *necessities*.

Again, the discipline you choose must be important to them! It must have an effect. Taking away television, but allowing them to keep their cell phones and computer time, is like taking only one of my five cookies from me.

How about when children behave badly in public, or even when there is just one other adult around? They still need to be disciplined. If you are at a store or in a restaurant and your children misbehave, get close to their face (you may need to grab them by the arm—firmly but not to hurt them), and explain some drastic consequences if the bad behavior continues. Then follow through. You can even pull them off to a corner or into the restroom and give *one* good spank, then hold them lovingly until they settle down.

If the behavior continues and does not look like it is going to stop, you may need to leave the store or restaurant with severe time out consequences or loss of privileges at home. Really, is any meal or shopping expedition more important than raising your children properly? Sometimes the discipline will come at a cost to you also, but it's worth it in the long run.

Consistent Discipline

Here is wonderful news! If parents start young and stay consistent with their discipline, I expect you will not have to discipline much past the age of eight or nine, maybe even younger. By that time—and with proper affection and guidance in all the other points discussed in this book—your children will know what the expectations are, they will want to please you, they will have internalized most of your values, they will act the way you want them to, and they will be who you expect them to be.

If you have not been disciplining well and you feel you have lost control of your children, here is what you can do. For children up to about seven years old, you can simply start disciplining them. It will be difficult for a while, but with perseverance you can do it, and they will catch on to the new way of living in your family. Your temptation will be to yell or lose your cool in some way. Just remain calm, tell them why they are being disciplined, and what the discipline will be—then do it! You *must do it*!

For eight- to eleven-year-olds, you will need to sit down with them and explain the changes. Try to be as specific as possible about expected behavior and the consequences for non-compliance. Address everything from language to hitting, and from schoolwork to bedtimes. As new situations come, sit down again and explain your expectations. At this age, you are still in complete control. State that these are your expectations and your disciplines.

But for twelve-year-olds and older, you may have to compromise some. You will need to have a full discussion about what is and what is not appropriate behavior. The reason you may need to compromise is that they might see this as a game in which they are trying to outwit you. Or they may become absolutely rebellious. Unless there is illegal or destructive behavior (drugs, alcohol, skipping school, vandalism …) going on, be happy to have a strong relationship with your child, share with her how much you love her and want the best for her, and keep the lines of communication open. With that said, it is still your house and your food, and he or she is still your son or daughter, and you should take control whenever it is warranted.

Finally, consistency is critical. Though grace is wonderful and even best at certain times, most bad behavior needs to be disciplined. Even a roll of the eyes should be addressed or it will very quickly turn into disrespect. If you tolerate bad language in some situations, your child will think it is fine under certain circumstances, which should not be the case. Cheating at a board game, if not checked, can lead to cheating in life that will have terrible consequences.

So be consistent! Discipline as often as needed. If you do this well at an early age, most children will not need long-term discipline.

Action Points

1. Write down a list of various creative disciplines you could use for each child. This is just for you and does not need to be shared with your child.

2. If your child consistently breaks one particular expectation, talk face to face with him and let him know the severe consequence of his actions in the future—then follow through!

CHAPTER 9

CENSOR THEIR LIVES

WHEN OUR CHILDREN were three and six, or maybe a year older, we took them to their first movie in a theater. We had built up the trip to be something very special. Going to the movies is no big deal anymore, but way back then and with our limited finances, this was a big deal. Deb and I rarely went to the movies, so we and the kids were all excited for the big day and a classic—*Lady and the Tramp*. What could be better than Disney!

Though I knew of the story, I don't think I had ever seen the movie. In an opening scene, the tough dogs are hanging around, talking like … tough dogs, and most of them are smoking. Both of our children started making comments: "Why are those dogs smoking?" "Gross!" "Those dogs are stupid."

Deb and I looked at each other, and she said, "I think we should leave." I am normally on the side of talking through things, using teachable moments, and thinking kids will forget things like this and get through it. But Deb was (and often is) wiser. We left the movie theater and didn't even get our money back—twenty dollars down the drain. Well, not exactly.

A few years later, Kyle returned from a friend's house because the friends decided to watch a PG-13 movie, and he knew he wasn't supposed to. A few more years later, we had moved and were trying to make new friends. We were at a new family's house for dinner. Kyle had gone downstairs with a couple older boys after dinner but came back and ended up hanging out with us around the dinner table. He didn't embarrass the family by saying anything, and we thought he just was shy and was having trouble relating. Later he told us that they were watching a funny movie—and then there were naked people. He knew what was appropriate and chose to leave the situation.

Katie doesn't deal well with scary movies and often called us up to pick her up early from a sleepover because of the direction the party was going. She also once found herself in a difficult situation at school with a substitute teacher who was acting inappropriately. She asked to be excused, found an administrator, and the problem was resolved—and the substitute was never asked back again.

Did walking out on that movie cause our children to act so bravely and appropriately? Yes . . . along with all the other things we chose to allow our kids to watch and not watch, to listen to and not listen to, and to play and not play.

Defining Ourselves

Try this word: no. We don't like this word very much. We don't like being told no, whether by a boss, a spouse, a company, a waiter, or a friend. We especially don't like it when our children say no to us. Those "terrible twos," which seem to last about four years, are full of no as a child struggles to define himself. They'll say no to ice cream just to prove they can do it.

And that is exactly what no does—it defines individuals and boundaries. Certainly yes defines us as well, but no does it more directly. We say yes to many things, like ice cream, movies, music, and traveling. But it is the no that gives us boundaries. Yes to ice cream, no to black raspberry (for me). Yes to movies, no to *Revenge of the Nerds*. Yes to music, no to The Chipmunk's Christmas Album. Yes to traveling, no to Siberia.

See how it works? We really do want to say yes to much of life, but there have to be limits. Yes to medicines, no to illegal drugs. Yes to parties, no to orgies. Yes to friends, no to bad influences. Yes to the television and the computer, no to the trash that can end up there.

Unfortunately, our society's children receive yes far too much, and many times without parents even knowing about it. We say yes when we really don't even know what is going on. This is true with the friends with whom they hang out, the activities in which they are involved, and especially the media they take in.

Censoring their lives does not mean always saying no. We say yes to most things in our children's lives. My concern is that too many parents say yes without having information. Or they have the information and aren't willing to say no. Or, even worse, they have the information and don't care or don't think these influences will affect their child.

Censoring begins with knowledge. And it begins with your own knowledge and your unique position to influence your children's lives. You know that young children should not watch violent television shows, shows with serious discussions about adult issues, or shows with sexual situations and innuendos. Because you know this, you should not allow your children to watch these shows or play video games with that content.

This means you need to know what they are watching and what is on the computer. And you should even limit the times they can do these activities so you can be sure they are not straying onto something they shouldn't see or hear. (This is a good reason for having early bedtimes.) If you don't want your children to be saying cuss words, then don't allow them to hear cuss words over and over on television, in movies, and in music. Know what your children are reading, watching, and listening to.

Important! Children today are not more mature than in the past—and your children are not more mature than others. Even if they are, they do not need to—and usually they can't—deal with the mature subject matter that most of them are being allowed to receive.

In the first chapter, I encouraged you to know as much about your children as possible. This is not just your right, but also your responsibility! Then, once you have that knowledge, you must do something with it. Usually that means saying no at some point.

This is probably the hardest part of parenting because of the peer pressure that both kids and parents feel. Because so few parents censor their children's lives, it's much harder for good parents to do it. And when they do, that makes their children feel like they are so different from others. So make sure your children know that different can be a very good thing. And because you love them, you are going to make sure they have the best life possible.

But which way should you approach this:

"I love you, *but* I'm not going to let you watch that movie." *Wrong.*

"I love you, *so* I'm not going to let you fill your mind with stuff that is not good for you." *Right.*

See the difference? Then keep explaining: "Our minds work so that those images or thoughts will stay with you—and I think they are not appropriate for your age." "It may be a funny movie, but the adult themes are subtle, and you will start thinking the way the television wants you to think."

Do children who watch *Halloween* movies grow up to kill their babysitters? Not usually. Do children who see a movie that includes divorce, when they grow up, hope that their marriage ends in divorce? I don't think so. But do these ideas become more acceptable? Yes.

Now let me give you three areas of concern that I have about what parents allow their children to do.

Media: Television, Movies, Music, and Video Games

At younger and younger ages, children are being allowed to watch just about everything. Certainly there is a problem when most children have seen PG-13 and R-rated movies by the time they are eleven. When Hollywood determines that children under a certain age should not be watching these movies, we should not go younger. If anything, we should go older! Hollywood is enticing younger children to watch these movies because they are "for older youth and adults." And children talk their parents into letting them watch them—often unsupervised.

Even if you think the movie does not have too much violence, bad language, or any sexual content, children should not have to be thinking about these adult themes. Complex ethical issues and adult relationships are not something with which an eleven-year-old has the cognitive ability to deal. "Teen" movies that highlight dating relationships and "love" are not the place where I want my pre-teen to learn. Yet this is exactly the audience that drives these TV shows and movies. And often, even if parents watch with their children, they fail to have an intelligent conversation about the issues afterward.

I once spoke with a family who had watched *Titanic* the night before with their fifteen-year-old and ten-year-old. With the whole family there, I asked if it was really an appropriate movie for their children. The parents said they skipped that one scene—to which the youngest child said, "Yeah, the sex scene in the back of the car." The children had either seen it at home without the parents' knowledge, seen it at another child's house, knew about it from conversations with other kids, or just plain figured it out by watching the movie. Any of those scenarios is bad. And even without the sex scene, that movie deals with things with which ten- (and possibly fifteen-) year-olds should not be concerned.

We didn't let our children watch many of the popular sitcoms because of the subtle messages they sent. *Friends* was a wonderfully funny show that often dealt with difficult relationship issues in a light-hearted but good way. But underlying the whole premise of the show was the idea that it was fun and even cool to go from one relationship to another, living together, without any long-term effects on the individuals and the relationships. This is simply not reality.

So even when we allowed our children to start watching the show as late teenagers, I still wanted to direct their thoughts. I had talks with them and often commented on the absurdity of this theme. They always jokingly mocked my "moralism," but they knew not to accept that part of the show while still enjoying the humor. Oh, and I'm 99 percent sure (I can't claim perfection) that neither of my children will sleep with anyone but their spouses—and not until they are married. And they are not missing anything—and they agree!

Music is so difficult to monitor because they have it on almost all the time—and it seems so harmless. Still, do everything you can to learn the music your children are listening to. You may need to look up the lyrics (easily done on the Internet) to learn what the songs say.

If you find questionable lyrics, you need to do something about it. For young children—take it away. For older children—take it away! For teens, get ready for a good talk about the things they put into their lives. Only you can determine what and how you can limit a teen's music choices. If you start young, as with discipline, this shouldn't be a problem. But if you are starting now, you at least need to have the conversation.

Start by quoting the questionable lyrics and asking your teen to explain them to you. This embarrassment (hearing you say these things, and their having to explain it) in itself ought to carry some weight! Then ask what they think about the lyrics. Is the topic something they think about? If so, could that be because they are listening to these lyrics? If you can't get rid of such music, keep having the conversations and pointing out the advantages of more positive music.

And video games. The sexy animes and the violence that is portrayed on many video games are not appropriate for children, and even young teens. I once overheard a conversation between thirteen-year-olds about a video game that they played not to see if they could win, but just to see this "hot babe" in her bikini over and over again. Adolescents fantasize enough—they don't need a video game to help them. And the violence is incredible. The link of violent crime to video games is still only anecdotal, but it just seems inappropriate for teens and children to be "playing" with such realistic violence.

Social Networking

I just read an article about the self-image difficulties that young teenagers are having because their friends don't comment each time they change their profile picture on Facebook. Yes, that is how teenagers think. That's why they change their profile picture. That's why they update their status so often. They want to know if anyone is paying attention to them! Of course, they would not believe this about themselves, but their own comments reveal this attitude.

Facebook, texting, and now even Twitter have popped up so quickly that most parents don't know what to do with them. You need to know they are not simply nice ways to stay in touch with friends. And most young people do not have the aptitude to understand what is at work with these networks. Being excited about your ten "BFFs" coming to your party just left out your other 247 friends. Most of those won't care, but there will be five to ten who will wonder why they were not invited.

People, especially teens, will write things on the Internet that they would never say in person. Then they are emboldened to say these same things in person. Such stray comments can easily destroy relationships. Most people have heard of cyber-bullying, where online tools are used to beat someone down using words—often copied by people who would never try to hurt the victim otherwise. And this is to say nothing of the language that's used and the potentially shocking topics that your child's three hundred closest friends talk about.

So wait as long as you can before allowing your teenager to have access to these networks. Tell them that you are not like other families that allow things that should not be allowed. Tell them you love them enough to say "no." And when you finally say "yes," monitor all of it. Make sure you are their "friend" on Facebook, you follow them on Twitter, and you check their texting if you start having concerns.

Excessive Freedom

Finally, I am concerned about young children being given far too much freedom with friends. I see third- and fourth-graders at high school football games, in amusement parks, at movies, at malls—just about everywhere—without any supervision. Parents may minimize the concern that something terrible could happen to their children—kidnapping, drugs, or basic immoral behavior.

But unsupervised children could also see things they shouldn't see. Underneath the stadium at a high school football game is one of the most eye-opening experiences someone can have. Most high school students have learned that public displays of affection are inappropriate. But junior high (middle school) students are just learning about the opposite gender and are not afraid to "go for it" wherever they are. In fact, they seem to revel in the thought (inappropriate as it may be) that they have a special friend and they get to touch each other in places that others don't. And children are under the stadium watching all this go on—and hearing the foul mouths. This is also true at malls and just about anywhere there are large crowds.

But there is an even more serious problem with letting children and young teens have too much freedom with each other. They are still learning values and morals. And usually their friends are not the best influence. Most often the worst person in the group is also the loudest—and an intimidator. Even good kids will be swayed by the intimidator and the mob mentality. Who is there to give direction for everything from manners to morals to values?

I recently went snow tubing with a group. The process is like skiing. You wait in line with several hundred people to get on the conveyor belt (instead of a lift) to take you to the top of the hill. Then you slide on a large inner tube down the hill and get in line again. The line is a little sloppy with people carrying their inner tubes and talking to each other. People don't mind if a friend or two cuts in line to be with another friend.

On this particular day, there was a group of about a dozen young boys, probably ten to twelve years old. I saw them do this once, but then they tried to do it again. After riding down the hill, they ran past several hundred people in line and jumped in front of some unsuspecting person near the front who was too busy in conversation to bother with them.

I stopped them in their tracks. "This is a line, guys. You need to go to the end."

They looked at me like I was from Mars. Then they looked at each other, wondering what to do. Most of the boys started to go to the back, but one stared me down—a pre-teen staring me down! How dare I mess up his day of cheating and make him look like a fool in front of his cronies! He finally gave in and headed to the rear of the line. And the line cheered!

These kids knew what they were doing was wrong, but they had no one there, no parent, to keep them in check. And this goes on everywhere. Children and teenagers will do whatever they think they can get away with—unless someone is there to show them the way.

It takes a very strong young person to go against the crowd. This is the role of parents. You need to be with your children and teenagers in more situations than you think—and for more years than you think. Manners, values, and morals need to be planted and replanted and cultivated as your children grow.

Don't think that they "have it" just because you taught them when they were young. Keep on teaching, modeling, and reinforcing for as long as you can. My son is married and twenty-four. Just last year he asked me about a difficult ethical issue he was facing.

My daughter is a wonderful twenty-one-year-old and is still dealing with some moral issues with which Deb and I are still directing her. Fortunately, we have always had a relationship with our kids that allows for these discussions—though many through the years have been difficult. We never stop training our kids. Even Deb and I still have to teach each other some things.

Action Points

1. Look up the lyrics to your child's or her friends' favorite musician's latest album.

2. Watch a TV show you have never seen but is popular with teenagers, even if your teen does not watch it.

CHAPTER 10

BE AN EXAMPLE

DO I REALLY need to write this chapter?

Most likely, your children will become like you. It's both genetic and cultural. Hopefully they will become better than we—mine certainly did! But your children will do what you do—and they can read you better than you think they can.

We can teach them not to lie and tell stories about how bad lying is. But if we ask them to tell the person on the phone that we are not there, all our talk is in vain.

If we tell them to go outside and play while we watch football games on TV all weekend, they will learn that as soon as they can decide for themselves, real life is found on the couch in the family room.

If we tell them they ought to read, but we never pick up the newspaper or a book, they will think of reading as a chore for students rather than an adventure and a great learning experience.

If you value faith in God, don't just send your children to the weekend gathering or even just go with them. You need to make your faith a part of every moment of your life. Otherwise, your children will leave it behind as just a religious exercise that has no effect on their lives.

What They Pick Up

When our son was about five, I remember going to the grocery store and walking hand in hand through the parking lot. There was a piece of trash in our path and I said, "Why do people throw trash on the ground, especially when there is a trash can fifty feet away?" And I picked up the trash. Next thing I knew (as my son led the way), we were roaming the parking lot, picking up trash wherever we could find it. All the while we talked about how bad it was to throw trash on the ground and why. To this day, I still hear Kyle say, "Why do people throw trash on the ground, especially when …" Word for word, what I said. As far as I know, neither of my children ever litter.

They learn it all from us. Our daughter, Katie, teaches with great passion, just like her mother. She is low key about many things, but when she starts talking about teaching, she lights up and speaks with enthusiasm. She got that from Deb. She also places a high value on play and what you can learn about life from playing. (Oh, yeah, I had a chapter on that.) So she is becoming a physical education teacher.

One final example. I am a graduate of Duke University. I received a great education there, but my continuing love for the school centers mainly around the basketball team. In case you don't follow college basketball, Duke's basketball program has been one of the very best for almost thirty years. Their famous coach, Mike Krzyzewski, has just become the all-time winningest coach at the Division 1 level, passing his mentor, Bob Knight. Many people hate Duke because it's a ritzy school with a squeaky clean image. I'm not naïve to think they don't have their problems, but it's my alma mater, so just get over it.

My children have never stepped onto the campus, not even close to it. They don't know the university president's name. They might not even be able to tell you the name of the city in North Carolina where the school is located. But one thing is for sure—they are avid Duke fans. And yes, I made sure of that! You may call it brainwashing; I call it influence. I never sat them down and told them they needed to be Duke fans. They just saw Deb and me, heard us talk about the games, and followed our lead.

The same is true for everything else. We don't cuss; they don't cuss. We like a certain kind of music; they like the same music. We work hard; they work hard.

It's called influence, and we have it in almost every aspect of their lives. Some people will say, "I want my child to learn on his own and not feel like he has to follow in my footsteps." That's fine for many things—hobbies, career choice, likes and dislikes—but it can't be true in all areas, especially those all-important morals and values.

Are you going to let your child decide for himself about taking illegal drugs? Is she allowed to depend on the lottery for income when she grows up? Is an obsession with Hitler and the Boston Strangler just as good as an obsession with Jesus or Gandhi? No. We have influence, and we ought to use it. And our greatest influence is through the way we live our own lives.

I'm not perfect—and I doubt you are either. Unfortunately, our kids will see all our imperfections and have to figure out the difference between our words and our actions. This is humbling.

My most visible faults are my lousy sleep habits and the fact that I eat too much junk food. There are times when I really work on each of these, but most of my adult life I have not been what I want my children to be—not even what *I* want to be! When they were young, I could get away with telling them what to do and hiding my issues. Certainly as teenagers, they could clearly see that I struggled in these areas. So as I worked on these habits, I was also absolutely honest with my kids. This did not excuse my behavior, but at least they understood that I was not being a hypocrite. I was simply being human. But I wanted them to avoid the problems I had because of these bad habits.

You do not need to tell them everything with which you struggle. But there will be areas where you are telling them one thing, maybe even disciplining them, and they are clearly seeing you do just the opposite. You must own this and be honest with them—or they will think that adults get to make up any rules they want in order to control their children. You need to communicate to your children that although you can't always follow your own rules and advice, you give them for the benefit of their whole life.

So be a good—*a great*—example for your children. Through all the teaching, rules, talk, play, love, discipline … realize they will most often do as you do. You have the privilege of forming them into wonderful children, and eventually, wonderful adults. This is the joy of parenting!

See, parenting is not all that hard. You simply need to love your children enough to do the right things—all the time. You can do it. Each day is a new beginning. You can begin right now. You do love your children. Put the effort into it—one day at a time. So go play with your son. Buy some apples instead of chips. Tuck your daughter into bed and spend a few minutes listening to her tell you about her day. Go find out what video game your son is playing (and try to beat him). Tell them and show them that no one loves them as much as you do.

Action Points

1. Change, even if it is just slightly, one of your own behaviors this week.

2. To develop self-control, go no faster than the speed limit everywhere you drive for a whole week.

APPENDIX

For parents who feel out of control

SOME OF YOU reading this book may already have older children or teenagers—and life is not going well. Your children might be rebellious, you may fear they are involved in some dangerous behaviors, or there is hardly any relationship. What do you do now since you do not have a good foundation from which to work?

First, do not think for a second that this will be easy. But you must do it! You love your child—and this is your chance to reconnect before he reaches adulthood. You want the very best for him. And whether you believe it or not, and whether he acts like it or not, you still have great influence on your child. You can make a difference—no matter how difficult the situation is.

First, ask … beg … bribe … whatever it takes, to get a full evening with your child. Plan to have her favorite meal or go to her favorite restaurant. But make sure you have time and privacy to talk. You might even take a walk in a park or just sit at a coffee shop. The key is that you won't be doing anything else and you won't have to be anywhere else so that the time is pressed. If there are two parents, both of you must be present. If there are problems throughout the family, make sure everyone is there. But if the problems are with only one child, meet only with that child. A teen will probably question the special attention. Tell her honestly that you need her help to be a better parent—and that this is about what she needs from you and not what you will demand of her.

If there are no real behavior problems, but you simply feel you are disconnected from your child, still have the special night together. Just go to steps 2, 10, 11, and 12 below.

1. Humble yourself. Tell her you feel you haven't done as good a job as you should have. Be specific: "I'm sorry I haven't been involved in your life." "We really never explained what our expectations were, then we just yelled and created a bad environment in our home." "I haven't said in such a long time how much I love you and how proud I am of you. I'm so sorry. I do love you so much." "When things started getting hard, I didn't know what to do and I feel like I just gave up."

2. Affirm your love for him. Tell him specifically what you like about him. Come prepared with lots of compliments. You can even write them down. Tell him that you didn't want to forget anything because you want him to know how truly special he is to you. Be sure to include physical attributes, accomplishments, talents, specific moments, and personality traits. "I remember last year when you let your friend get all the credit for something you did too. I really admired you for that." Also include special

times you had together—vacations, ball games, silly moments—even if they were years ago. And then tell him how much you want to have special moments again. This may end up being the longest part of the evening if you both start reminiscing and he starts to truly feel your love for him. That would be a good thing.

3. Share the principles of the first chapter of this book. Again, the emphasis is on how much you love her, so you want to do everything you can to make sure she has the best opportunities for a wonderful life. And it is not only your *desire*, it is your *responsibility* to work for this.

4. Ask him what he thinks could work better in your home or in your relationship. Then listen. He may have some very good points that should direct the rest of your conversation. Just be sure from this point on that you don't blame him or try to defend yourself. Admit even the smallest truths. You are rebuilding trust.

5. Figure out—between the items she brings up and the areas about which you are most concerned—what should be worked on and what can wait. Most likely, the battle is past for eating habits (chapter 3) and reading habits (chapter 5). (If your child truly has an eating disorder or is becoming obese, you need to get your family physician involved.) The items that are fully your responsibility are playing with her (being involved in her life—chapter 4), affirming her (chapter 7), and being an example (chapter 10). And talking with her (chapter 6) stems from all the other basics. So, most likely, the key areas will be privacy

(chapter 1), setting a bedtime (chapter 2), discipline (chapter 8), and censoring her life (chapter 9).

6. Don't try to work on ten different items, just the key areas that both of you agree are problems. A rebellious teen who is out of your control will probably say she likes things the way they are. If this is the case, state firmly, but with great love, how you cannot allow things to continue the way they are—because you love her too much to accept where her life is headed.

7. Be ready to compromise. If his grades stay up, he doesn't act out or disrespectfully, and he doesn't fall asleep during the day, then the bedtime can stay the same. He can watch certain shows, but only if you watch with him. Together, figure out appropriate disciplines for behaviors about which you are concerned.

8. For serious behavior problems, make it clear that there will be no compromise and that the discipline will be severe. These problems would include skipping school, fighting, alcohol and other drug use, vandalism, and obstinate disobedience. (Many of these are not just behavior issues; they are also legal issues.) And severe consequences would include extensive grounding; taking away the car, cell phone, and other electronics; and missing concerts, dances, dates … remember, it needs to reach her heart and have a great effect.

9. Inform him that within a month (he deserves a chance to clear out any embarrassing items) you will have the right and responsibility to go through his room, backpack, car, and whatever else he used to think was only his. Remind him that this is because

of your great love for him. You may want to even read the first chapter to him and ask if this makes sense. Reaffirm your love for him throughout this process. He has to know this is not about punishment, but about love, his best interests, and your relationship with him. And reassure him that if his behavior is appropriate, there will be no reason for you to check out his stuff. It is your hope that you never have to resort to this invasion of his privacy. And be true to this. Be sure to remain calm throughout this discussion, even if he starts to get upset. He will try to push your buttons. But eventually he will handle this just the way you do. So be an example of how to have this "adult" conversation.

10. Listen. And no advice! You are still earning the right and trust to give advice. Admit again that you are so sorry that your relationship with her is not what you want it to be. Then get her talking. "So tell me about life now. What do you love? What do you hate? Who is your best friend? Why? What do like about school? Where is your favorite place to hang out? Do you have any fears? Do you think about what you might want to do when you get out of school? What do you like best about yourself?" As you listen, you will hear what she wants to talk about. Go with that. Just keep listening. Don't add too many of your own stories, even if you are just trying to relate. Remember, this is all about her, not you. Even if she asks for advice, give her great respect by saying, "I have some ideas, but what do you think?" Then continue the discussion. Resist absolutes. Allow for disagreement, but show her that you will always love her and that you understand that some things are

really difficult to figure out. This is not about the right answer; it's about your building a relationship with her. Listen. Listen. Listen.

11. And finally, play with him—get involved in his life. Without being intrusive, show up at everything you can—the game, the play, the concert. Ask to play tennis, toss a ball, or go for a walk. Listen to him practice his instrument. Ask how the test went. Knock on his bedroom door and ask what music he is listening to. Sit with him for a few minutes and talk about the music, then exit just as easily. (No harsh judgments allowed!) Have a movie night together—at home or at the theater. Do these things over and over again, week after week, month after month, and the talking will improve, the respect will return, and the love will grow. And why wouldn't you do these things—you love your child!

12. Ask … beg … bribe again to have another meal or evening together next week, because you really miss her and really love her, and you really want to get this right. It's just one night. But hopefully it will turn into two or three every week, because she will love you just as much!

CPSIA information can be obtained at www.ICGtesting.com
Printed in the USA
BVOW031903050213

312483BV00003B/6/P